The Light

The Light

A Poetry Collection

Zaria Alia

RESOURCE *Publications* · Eugene, Oregon

THE LIGHT
A Poetry Collection

Copyright © 2021 Zaria Alia. All rights reserved. Except for brief quotations in critical publications or reviews, no part of this book may be reproduced in any manner without prior written permission from the publisher. Write: Permissions, Wipf and Stock Publishers, 199 W. 8th Ave., Suite 3, Eugene, OR 97401.

Resource Publications
An Imprint of Wipf and Stock Publishers
199 W. 8th Ave., Suite 3
Eugene, OR 97401

www.wipfandstock.com

PAPERBACK ISBN: 978-1-6667-3028-9
HARDCOVER ISBN: 978-1-6667-2156-0
EBOOK ISBN: 978-1-6667-2157-7

NOVEMBER 2, 2021

Scripture quotations marked NLT are taken from the *Holy Bible*, New Living Translation, copyright © 1996, 2004, 2015 by Tyndale House Foundation. Used by permission of Tyndale House Publishers, Inc., Carol Stream, Illinois 60188. All rights reserved.

Scripture taken from the New King James Version®. Copyright © 1982 by Thomas Nelson, Inc. Used by permission. All rights reserved.

The Word.
the Word gave life
to everything that was created
and His life brought light
to everyone.

the light shines in the darkness,
and the darkness can never
extinguish it.
JOHN 1:4–5 NLT

Contents

A Message | ix

1 Healing and Learning

Old Friend | 3
Self-Talk 1,2,3 | 4
Things Unseen | 5
A Caged Bird | 7
Forgiveness | 8
Think First | 10
Run Away | 12
Finish Her | 14
Fear | 15
Mosaic | 16
Sometimes I Have to Remind Myself | 17
Brokenness | 18

2 A Shift

A Decision | 21
Freedom | 22
So, this is What Peace Feels Like | 23
Introduce Me to Myself | 24
An Answered Cry | 25
Identity | 26
Good as dead? | 27

Ordered Steps | 28
Bloom | 29
Adventure | 30
The Wind | 31
Freed | 32
I Fell in Love | 33

3   LOVE

As You Love Yourself | 37
Hurt People | 38
Happily, Ever After? | 39
Love | 41
Always and Forever | 42

4   SECRET PLACE

Who Are You? | 45
Creation | 46
He Wasn't There | 47
You Are | 49
Perfection | 50
The Potter Who Knew | 51
Desperation | 52
There is a Call | 53
Sacrifice | 55
Relationship | 56
Favor | 57
Life | 58
Praise | 59
The Highest Praise | 60
Things He has, things He does, who He is | 62

A Message

this is the first of its kind,
for the first of their kind.
my God-given helpers,
my family by choice.
this book is dedicated to God but would not have
happened without your consistent love and support.
thank you.
even though these words are not enough.

now to the reader,
I pray this blesses you,
that it inspires you,
and most of all,
that God be glorified.

enjoy.

all the love,

Zaria

1

Healing and Learning

Old Friend

my sadness is like an old friend.
someone who hurt you,
but you haven't seen them for a while so,
you forget.

you let them back in
when they come around again;
and once they're back,
you remember why
they were an old friend
in the first place.

but habits die hard
and they're back now,
do I let them stay?

it's nice to see a familiar face.

Self-Talk 1,2,3

send smiles,
send heart eyes,
end your sentences with exclamation marks.
happy tone,
they can't know,
catch your breath,
don't you dare fall apart,
not here, not now
get it together,
keep it together
do. not. explode.

someone's coming.
1, 2, 3 . . . smile.

Things Unseen

I went back home to look in the mirror.
at first, I didn't understand why.
I thought it would ground me,
remind me of who I am.

really, I was looking for proof.
any physical sign of the pain I was in;
the pain I was putting myself through.

I thought about how I would never hurt
anyone else in my life
as much as I hurt myself.
I would never treat someone I love
the way I treat myself.

except, maybe I would,
maybe I had.
although fully aware,
I would have myself believe it was
unintentional.

I've been trying to love myself for a long time
but the learning curve is steeper than I expected.
I keep tripping and somehow falling
all the way back down into numbness.

I bought what I wanted,
shopped where I wanted,
ate what I wanted.
I treated myself.

but I didn't do the work,
I wasn't worth that much energy.
layers of superficial treatment
would eventually put the depth of the brokenness
to the back of my mind where I made space for it.

I knew faith was made of things unseen,
but when I looked in the mirror,
I couldn't see this either.

A Caged Bird

tell me about a caged bird.
if you feed it, it will grow,
its wings will become
long and strong.
it becomes sure of its home,
sure of its safety,
surrounded by familiarity.

the caged bird is wise,
it knows the sunrise and
wakes up with the daylight.
it knows when to eat, when to speak
and when to keep quiet.

but there is one thing it will
never know;
the feeling of the free air of the sky,
with no cage to keep it at the same height.
is this a haven or a prison?
a caged bird will never know how high it can fly as long as
they are kept inside.

Forgiveness

why choose to hold on to the
things that hurt you?
when you can give them to me?
my hand is stretched toward you,
and I ask you gently to let it go.
you say you forgive,
you say you forget,
I prepare for you to hand it to me
but you hold on.

I'll try a new approach.
I hold your hand and look at you,
again, you say you forgive,
again, you say you forget.
this time you reach your hand toward me,
you hold it open, close your eyes
and say please, take it away.
before you change your mind,
I take the weight from your hand.
tears are okay,
I'll wipe them away.
I don't let go of your hand and
I tell you that I'm proud of you.
For trusting me
more than your pain,
trusting me
more than your anger.

this is the best decision
you could have made.
now I have space
to teach you,
to mold you.
by letting go,
you have allowed me
to set you free.

Think First

make sure that every word
you speak in a day
is something that you desire
to create.

when you let the words
leave your mouth
that you are not strong enough,
when you confess that an obstacle
is too hard,
or a wall too high;

you create a space where
the things you want are not able to manifest.
you destroy them,
defeating yourself
before you could even try.
a slip of the tongue is a luxury
you do not have.

every word is heard, registered
and formed.
measure your speech carefully,
think first.
taking care not to be careless
with the authority you carry.
passing by some conversations
in silence;

because there are some situations
that have not earned
the value of your voice.

Run Away

run away.
run far, far away
as fast as you can
run, runaway.

wait,
you think you've gone too far
and you can't recognize
where you are.
the distance
doesn't silence the voices;
they're just as loud as they were
when you left the place
you thought was your prison.

but you already started running,
keep going.
your legs hurt,
you try to ignore it.
one step in front of the other,
each step less certain than the last.

where are you going?
you don't know.
what are you running from?
the battle in your mind?
that's not a battle you run from,
that's the kind you have to fight.

how?
listen to the voice sent by those
who love you
saying stop, breathe,
and turn around;
come to yourself.
take one step in the right direction
and you won't have to
run anymore.

there is a Father waiting
with open arms,
not too far away;
while you were running
He chased.

to wrap you in His love
and bring peace to the storm.
so, take a deep breath,
let love have its way,
let Him give you strength
to run the right race.

Finish Her

if someone runs away from a problem,
runs away from a fight,
sees their opponent and
turns the opposite way,
thinking they're better off
not engaging in the battle,
did they win?
it's not rhetorical;
if you run away, do you win?

you forfeit.

the beautiful battle scars, the badges of honor
that could have been yours,
you turn away from.
now here lies someone else's heart in your hand,
struggling to stay together.
they trust you with their heart
because you know this battle.
but you didn't fight it.
now the heart that you hold that is waiting to be told
the strategy to overcome,
finds themselves being led to battle
by someone who has never fought,
never won.
choose to fight, choose to stand,
though it may not feel worth it,
the victory is not just for you.

Fear

don't choke or fail,
don't slip or fall,
don't try, stay here;
your comfort zone.
why even bother?

constantly speaking the opposite of what God wills,
convincing us that we aren't good enough,
not strong enough, not worthy.

but He gave us power,
He gave us love and a sound mind,
so, fear is nothing but
the voice of the enemy playing on our own anxiety,
waiting for us to arise and silence it
with faith, with love,
with the Word of God;
who is the only One you should ever fear.
with confidence in Him I say,
I am no longer afraid.

Mosaic

I've lived a broken life,
hurting.
choosing pain over healing every time.
ever since I could remember,
there has been so much brokenness.
I thought I didn't deserve to be whole.
I truly believed that being shattered
was all that life had to offer.
it made me feel ugly.
I thought being hurt was something
to be ashamed of,
something to run away from.
people always say to find
the beauty in the pain.
but all I felt, all I saw, was darkness,
and torment.
but God is so creative,
He can take broken pieces and make them
into something magnificent;
like a mosaic,
carefully placed back together.
once broken, now whole.
maybe not put together the same way,
but beautiful, nonetheless.

Sometimes I Have to Remind Myself

I'm not losing my mind.
I'm not depressed.
I'm just on my way, still processing,
and that is okay.

Brokenness

I looked for it in the wrong places, I'm so glad I found it
in You.
it's raw, it's real, it's true.
temptation comes,
but what the world has to offer
does not compare
to what I have with You.
open and vulnerable,
I didn't know what transparency was
until I met You.

with You, honesty is not an option,
it's a requirement.
I face You
and I have to face myself.
it hurts, it's the truth,
but it's a good pain, the healing kind.
broken no longer, except to You.

2

A Shift

A Decision

today, I decided to fight.
today, I decided that my life is worth fighting for.
today, I decided no longer to go in whichever direction
the wind in this storm pushes me.
not anymore.
I look my demons in their eyes
and I tell them that I have had enough.
this ends today.

Freedom

before I knew it,
I could breathe.
before I knew it,
love rushed in where only darkness lived.
now the light shines and it can never be extinguished.

So, this is What Peace Feels Like

I found my place of being
when my spirit became stronger than my mind.
when peace became more than a concept,
it became a way of living,
ingrained into my DNA.

although the world around me
may have been crumbling into chaos,
although naturally it would have made sense
to start feeling like nothing makes sense anymore,

I focused on one thing.
I focused on You,
and You kept me at peace.

Introduce Me to Myself

help me.
I think I know who I am,
but I am so easily swayed,
so easily discouraged.
if I know who I am, why don't I have confidence?
confidence that lasts.
every time I think I've overcome this,
comparison comes to poison my thoughts,
or doubt, or fear.
so, help me.
I'm starting to believe that You know me better than I do.
show me who You think I am.
I'd love to get to know her.

An Answered Cry

You hear me when I cry out in silence,
to others there is no sound.
but, to You it must be so loud,
because there's a voice inside, a desperation,
that always has to break out.
it keeps me moving stops me from staying in this dark place,
rescues me from being so accustomed to the pain.
You hear, You come,
You hold, You heal.
my home, my happy place.
my forever.
the One who's always there
to hold me together.

Identity

who am I?
a question I ask myself often,
especially in times of self-doubt
and when mistakes are made.
He reminds me of who I am.
I am, simply, loved.
loved by Him in an undeserving, infinite way.
love is who He is
and I belong to Him;
loved is who I am.

Good as dead?

from death, to life.
no matter how far you think you've gone,
how dead you may be on the inside,
His resurrection power
can bring you back to life.
turn that cold death into a bright fire
that spreads to those around you.
good as dead?
He'll still use you.

Ordered Steps

it is He who brings every stone into place,
so that we have a path to walk on.
don't think you could keep walking,
or keep moving forward without Him.
every step you are able to take
is only by His grace.

Bloom

every flower takes a different length of time to blossom.
there's a period of hiding,
a period of piercing through the ground,
a period of growing
and an abundance of rain
before a flower blooms to take on its full beautiful and
colorful form.

God takes his time with those He loves
to make sure every petal is in the perfect place.

just because someone doesn't see your value,
doesn't mean it's not there.

God knows exactly how and when He needs you to bloom.
if they step on you, He will rebuild you,
because you are loved.

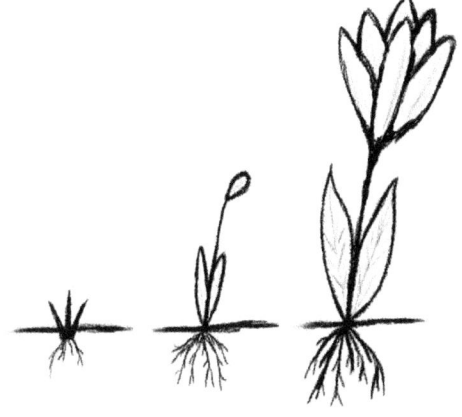

Adventure

don't be afraid to jump in,
to say yes, to embrace
to run before you walk,
to explore or to chase.

fall in love,
escape,
do something you've never done.
try something new.

today I stopped to look at the flowers.
I made my way to a known destination on a known path
and discovered some unknown things along the way.

flowers are prettier in person.
they don't all look the same,
some stand tall,
while some slouch a little.
birds communicate in song.
the clouds and trees shield you from the sun,
making you more aware of the wind.

where does the wind come from?
where does it go?

The Wind

the wind blows where it wishes,
and you hear the sound of it,
but cannot tell where it comes from and where it goes.

John 3:8 NKJV

Freed

I am what most would call a free spirit.
but I am not a free spirit;
I am a freed spirit.
for whom the Son sets free, is free indeed.
now I am no longer trying my hardest to stay within
the lines of the box that society drew for me.
no, I will not conform to the ways of this world.
for I have been set free.
free to live the life the living word, Jesus, wrote for me
and so, from the world, I am freed.
free to belong to something greater,
free to be one with my Creator.
free to take on an easy yoke, and a light burden.
it's counterintuitive for sure,
that someone who was set free
would then choose to be bound,
a prisoner.
but, a prisoner of Christ is no prisoner at all.
for through Him, I can do all things.

I Fell in Love

I fell in love with art
when I sat down on the ground outside one day,
looked up and realized
that the clouds in the sunset looked like an artist's brush
strokes.

the sky was pink, orange and purple.
I had admired it before,
because blue skies and sunlight make you feel like
you've had a perfect day before it's even started.
but there was something special about the sky
being so many colors at the same time.

I fell in love when I learned that the sky isn't always blue,
but it is always beautiful.

eventually, in the hardest of seasons,
I learned to find beauty in the grey too.

I couldn't always count on clear skies.
sometimes I couldn't count on the energy
to get up, go outside and look up.
but there was beauty in all of it.

there was beauty in the joy,
beauty in the turmoil and the pain,
beauty in the days I couldn't feel anything,
and beauty in the days I managed to feel it all.

I fell in love with art when I realized
I was free to be honest.
art values honesty, and even if it isn't what people expect it to be,
there is beauty in it all.

3

Love

As You Love Yourself

I look at myself in the mirror.
and choke on the words.
I've never said them to myself,
so, I don't recognize this feeling.
something on the inside of me starts to break,
or maybe I was already broken.
I try again to say what I know I need to hear,
But I can only muster silent tears.

I close my eyes,
not wanting to see myself fall apart.
but it needs to be said until I believe it,
until it's the truth.
ready?
I love myself.

Hurt People

open wounds, hidden baggage,
ignored pain, forced smiles,
distractions.
fall in love,
lose themselves.
found again,
broken, and breaking others,
oblivious to their need for healing.
spreading their hurt wherever they go.
using anything, anyone
to make them feel whole.

shattered,
attracting attention,
jagged edges piercing the people
that try to put them back together.
one person is hurt,
and hurts another.
two people are hurt,
and hurt two others.

Happily, Ever After?

there could never be too many, not ever enough.
the hopeless romantic in us longs to know
the story of the new boy meeting a new girl,
falling so in love that they forget the whole world.
reality's suspended, they're on cloud 9,
their connection is a force
that slows down time.

but, the honeymoon ends
and panic sets into their eyes,
when they realize
that time only slowed down in their minds.
the world is still moving, they have to face life;
make decisions, work smart,
and try hard to be wise.

thoughts regress from us to we,
those who loved now cause pain,
as they withdraw passively.
tears flow, and you cry too,
as it reminds you of a love
that you had to lose.

why do we seek
to immerse ourselves
in the thing that hurt us so badly in the first place?
adjusting our palates to ignore the bitter in bittersweet.
reminiscing so long that we get lost in our minds,
trying to bring the past into the present.

the story picks up and the smiles return.
the smiles turn to laughter
and the comfort of familiarity creeps in.
we watch our boy and our girl
go from believing they have to leave,
to being too afraid to do anything but stay.

what if happy ever after is just the fear of the unknown,
pushing you to stay where it's safe?
mistaking comfort for love.

what if they didn't run towards each other in the rain
and instead, remained apart.
discovering that there is something better for them,
if for a little while, they could be okay with being
uncomfortable.

real life isn't as entertaining as a love story.
it can be boring; it hurts and there's much less to tell.
so, we wait until another story comes around.
so, we can enjoy the rollercoaster of emotions again.
a new boy,
a new girl,
a new love,
in a made-up world.
broken fantasies,
broken hearts,
pain, tears, smiles, laughter,
reunite;
happily, ever after?

Love

I will never understand,
but will always cherish
the unconditional nature of His love.
for He is love
and He has no end,
so, He gives love without end.

He will always chase you, the one,
even if He has to leave the ninety-nine
an infinite number of times.
grace that is to be honored,
a lover is who He is,
and for who He is,
the highest praise should be given.
never taken for granted,
but requiring eternal gratitude,
because His love is poured undeservedly
and consistently every single time.

Always and Forever

this type of love
is not the kind you find
looking for it too hard.
it sneaks up on you,
when you are at your lowest
and there is only one person you want to talk to.
only one who can comfort you.
some spend their lives searching for it,
so, it must be cherished.
it is a promise,
surpassing a lifetime;
always and forever.

4

SECRET PLACE

Who Are You?

show me who You are.
I would give anything to see the face
of the One who created me,
the One who wrote my story.
please, if I am found worthy,
show me Your glory.
not so I can tell anyone I have seen it,
but because every atom,
everything that I am cries out,
yearning to know who You are.
that's all I want to know.
that's what I want to see.
who are You?

Creation

with His words,
He spoke every fiber into existence.
every droplet of water,
every leaf,
every beast,
every tree.

all flowing in the cadence of His praise.
all obeying that still, small voice,
the whisper of His instruction.

He has given this authority to His children,
to His sheep,
to command everything on this Earth.
to speak and watch our words create
exactly what we want to see.
decree a thing and it shall be.
we were not just created to rule,
we were created to create.

He Wasn't There

He wasn't there.
they went to mourn,
they went to weep,
to face their defeat.
but,
He wasn't there.
they looked,
but the tomb they laid Him in was empty,
nothing but linen left in His place.

sadness deepened,
confusion set in,
any chance of closure slowly slipped away,
what have they done with my Lord?

but then appeared two messengers,
angels of the Lord;
there is no reason to weep.
behold, a teacher
and a conqueror.
the only one who conquered the grave,
so, the highest power would be in His name.

here to give the ultimate gift,
to complete the trinity
Father, Son, now the Holy Spirit.
with His breath He sent us,
as He was sent,
now we too have power over death.

all hail the King of kings,
all hail the Lord of lords.
ascended to His throne at the right hand,
where He will reign forevermore.
He's alive.
sin and death are destroyed
because of His sacrifice.
hell has no power over me,
for the One who lives still has the keys.
now all creation has been set free,
because,
He wasn't there.

You Are

You are there,
here,
in no particular direction.

You are with me,
within me,
around me.

You are.
You just are.
everything to me.
everywhere,
born, dead, now alive.
You have been,
You are
and You will be
forevermore.

Perfection

nonexistent to the natural mind,
abundant in His holiness.
the harmony of three in one,
poured out in His perfect love.
always knowing what to say,
always knowing what you need.

if harm ever comes your way,
He will be your sword,
and your shield.
perfection only exists
in the One
who is the living word embodied,
who was and is to come.

every moment planned,
every step ordered.
rest,
knowing you are not perfect,
but He is.

The Potter Who Knew

carefully formed,
carefully planned,
fully known,
wonderfully made.
soft clay in the safe hands of the potter,
who breathed life into dust
and gave it a name.
spoke a word,
a purpose
that will not return to Him void.

ignited a passion
as a direction,
an infinite flame
He continues to tend
with the care of a Father;
an unconditional love.

so, silence fear,
cancel doubt,
and when the lies build
and the voices get loud,
remember this simple truth;
He placed all of Him inside of you
and He knew you before you were formed in the womb.

Desperation

when you want nothing more
than to be with Him.
when more is never enough.
a thirst, a hunger,
a deep yearning
in the depths of your soul,
that only the infinity
and endlessness of His presence
could possibly satisfy.
a constant reminder that He is your first love,
that He is your Only.

There is a Call

arise all who are dead to self,
all who have been consumed by the fire of life.

He who is alive and lives in us,
calls us to our true being.
when He died,
so did our sin,
we are reborn,
we are made clean.

there is a call to manifest,
creation waits to hear the sound
of His glory springing out
from His sons and daughters
and that time is now.

there is a call,
for all who have surrendered
to walk this Earth as its light.

there is a call,
from shepherd to sheep
to all who are listening.

there is a call,
we will not wait any longer,
it is our time to manifest.

there is a call,
Lord, from the depths of our hearts,
we cry a resounding yes.

Sacrifice

He desires a sacrifice.
reasonable worship.
not living for myself,
living for Him.
where does He want me to go?
what does He want me to do?
what does He want me to say?

I hear, listen, and obey,
because I was purchased,
at the highest price;
the blood of Jesus,
the ultimate sacrifice.
so, this is His life,
not mine.
not I who lives,
but Jesus Christ.

Relationship

when you cling to Him on the bad days,
just as much as the good ones.
when He is the first person you can open up to;
vulnerability, intimacy, comfort.
a Father,
a great friend,
and a lover all the same.
all encompassing,
exactly who you need Him to be
whenever you need Him,
so, why turn away?
turn to Him,
He's always there anyway.
He promised He would never leave.
it's a relationship,
a two-way street.

Favor

how could someone
who is infinite,
who is all powerful,
think of me and decide
I should always be by His side,
and Him by mine.

goodness that cannot be explained,
fueled by love,
covers shame.
favor.

Life

You are Life,
that's why You can give it.

omnipresent,
occupying all space.
every breath,
every tear,
even every thought.
I am alive in You
and You are alive in me.
living water,
breath of life,
You are alive.
You are Life.

Praise

one thing you must understand about praise,
is that it cannot be contained.
it pierces through the atmosphere,
through the dark clouds,
allowing light to enter.

it flows straight to the throne,
creating a place
where the One who is too Holy
for anyone to see,
can come and dwell among us.

The Highest Praise

in an attempt to thank You,
in an attempt to bring You
an offering of praise and worship
that is worthy enough
to demonstrate what You deserve;

I begin to understand
the necessity of angels singing Hosanna.
the need for living creatures
singing of Your holiness,
declaring that to You alone
is all glory, all honor and all power.

for what praise could embody
greatness of this magnitude?
what song could do justice
to Your glorious presence?

all praise will never be enough,
so, eternity will praise You.
the highest praise,
our best, our everything,
is what we offer.

to add to the eternal adoration You deserve.
to add to the never-ending song,
the endless outpouring of worship
that is brought to Your throne.

in the comprehension
of Your majesty,
there is nothing left to say,
but Hallelujah,
the highest praise.

Things He has, things He does, who He is

seven stars,
seven lamps,
sevenfold,
perfection.

missing nothing,
holding everything,
filling all things.

jealous,
love,
hating evil,
giver of victory.

tree of life,
first and last,
resurrected,
still to come.

two-edged sword,
man of war,
fiery eyes,
feet of brass.

all-knowing,
all powerful,
the beginning and
The End.

www.ingramcontent.com/pod-product-compliance
Lightning Source LLC
Chambersburg PA
CBHW061508040426
42450CB00008B/1529